More Exciting Than a Throne Speech!

More Powerful Than a Minister Without Fort Polio!

More Controversial Than Metrication!

Humbler Than Pierre Elliott Trudeau!

Sexier Than Joe Clark!

Funnier Than Rene Levesque!

More Baffling Than Margaret Trudeau's Whereabouts!

This book ought to stop Canadians from asking Americans what they think of Canada —

Because this American really tells you.

Here, for the first time, is the definitive Canadian joke — 500 of them — almost one for every person in the country.

If you think THIS is bad, you should see my marriage!

The Retarded Giant

by Bill Mann

Introducing
the definitive
Canadian joke

Drawings by Aislin

Tundra Books 1977

Tundra Books of Montreal
Montreal, Quebec   H3G 1J6
ISBN 0-88776-095-3

Printed in Canada.

FOREWORD

I mean, fair's fair, right? Those Canucks down at the
National Lampoon in New York have been making their
living for years ripping apart the U.S., so why shouldn't a
Yank living up here be able to do the reverse? Besides,
Canadians are the world's consummate straight men, and I
couldn't move to Los Angeles until I put these jokes
together.

The in-joke among Yanks living up here has always been,
"Wouldn't you rather be a big fish in a small pond than the
reverse? " Actually, no, but it was the weather that finally
did me in. The weather WILL keep Canada out of the big
time.

I know that Canadians like to laugh about as much as most
people like to pull nose hairs, but even if most Canucks don't
find this book funny, at least I will have left the legacy of
the Canadian joke (see first chapter). Besides, I didn't have
any season tickets to leave.

You aren't gonna find any Newfie jokes in here, though,
because: 1) books — many books — are already full of them,
and 2) they're nothing but warmed-over Polish jokes
anyway. Thanks again to the Canucks at the *National
Lampoon* who gave me the idea for the book (and the
title).

In all generosity to Canada, I haven't put one joke about the
black flies in the entire book!

To paraphrase Roy and Dale, happy snowmobile trails.

— Bill Mann
Montreal, March 1977

To Jean, whom I would have married anyway, even if she hadn't been a great manuscript typist; and to little Floyd, who tried his mightiest to tear up every chapter. Maybe he knew something.

Also, thanks to Sean Kelly and all the other Canucks at the National Lampoon *who gave me the idea for the title; and special thanks to Terry (The Nose Knows) Mosher.*

TABLE OF CONTENTS

MANN'S CANADIANIZED QUOTATIONS

→ BE SOMEWHAT DECISIVE.
→ DRIVE A METEOR.
→ EAT SPAGHETTI WITH A HOCKEY STICK.
→ DRINK NIAGARA PORT OUT OF A MOCCASIN.

Q. Why do Canucks end their sentences with "eh? "?
A. To see if their listener is awake.

1. Introducing: The Canadian Joke

Q. How can you recognize a Canadian at a party?
A. When he comes in, it seems like someone just left.

*A Canadian was taking a routine word association test in
the office of his plant psychologist.*
"Body," said the doctor.
"...by Fisher," replied the Canuck.
"Vagina," came the next question.
"Alberta? "

Q. Why does a haircut in Canada cost four dollars?
A. A buck for each corner.

*Son on long distance to father in Toronto: "Dad, Margaret
and I have great news for you! We're engaged."*
Father: "In what? "

Some Canadian conversation-stoppers:
"My brother knows Beryl Plumptre's accountant! "
"Ladies and gentlemen, the Lieutenant-General! "
"I once was on the same CP Air flight with Pierre Berton! "
"Last year, we had no snow on the ground until NOVEMBER! "

Q. What are things Canadians don't have to worry about encountering?
A. Monsoons, earthquakes, volcanoes, heat prostration, and interesting conversation.

Overheard in a Halifax bar: "Can I buy you boys a drink, or would you like the cash? "

Q. What do Canadians have in common with U.S. Army generals?
A. They always miss the Point.

Speak softly and carry a big megaphone.

A Canadian woman who had just moved to Chicago asked her American boyfriend, "Where do you find a good gynecologist in this town? "
Her boyfriend chuckled, "I'll look into it for you."
"Please do," she answered, walking away. "And call when you've got a name."

Q. What's "Canada" spelled backwards?

A. Very appropriate.

An indigent walks up to a stranger on the street in Toronto and asks, "Could I please have a quarter for a sandwich?" The Canadian replies: "First, show me the sandwich..."

American: "How do you keep a Canadian in suspense?"
Canadian: "How?"
American (chuckling): "I'll tell you tomorrow!"
Canadian: "Please do."

"Do you have frog legs?" the American tourist joked to the waiter in a Vancouver restaurant.
"Yes," the waiter replied.

> *Jack and Jill went up the hill/to fetch a pail of water/Jack fell down, and broke his crown/and so he immediately phoned his dentist.*

Q. What's the next career advancement after you've had your own CBC show?

A. You read the Quickie Special announcements on the P.A. at Miracle Mart.

A Canadian wife shows her husband her new, transparent negligee. "How do you like it?" she asks him.
"Fine," he replies, "but is it non-flammable?"

WHAT IS THE QUEEN'S MAJOR ROLE IN CANADA?
☐ a figurehead?
☐ a loggerhead?
☐ she sells lots of stamps.

Q. Why are Canadians such a proud people?
A. That's a good question...

Q. What is news in Canada?
A. Anything.

Q. How can you tell Canadians are stuffy?
A. In Canada, the marching bands have cellos.

Q. What does a Canadian lawyer call a document 30 pages long?
A. A "brief."

Q. What's the hardest thing to get a Canadian to do?
A. Bet $10 on a sure thing.

Q. What's the most popular oral contraceptive in Canada?
A. The word "no."

Q. What do you call a traffic accident in Canada?
A. "Entertainment."

Q. Why does a Canadian usually go to a massage parlor?
A. To get a back rub.

(A Canadian variation on an old joke)
A Canadian was driving in a sleazy part of town, when he ran a red light. The cop pulled him over and asked, "Didn't you see the red light?"
The Canadian replied, "I didn't even see the amber."

Q. What's the one thing that makes most Canadians laugh?
A. A natural disaster in Quebec.

Q. Give three examples of "contradictory terms."
A. Military intelligence; Catholic university; Canadian humor.

Q. What can you do about a guy who insists he likes Hamilton?
A. Poison his dog or steal his white cane.

First Canadian (slyly and knowingly): "Who was that lady I saw you with last night? "
Second Canadian: "That was my wife."

An American wanted to try out a new joke he'd heard on his Canadian friend.
"Knock, knock," said the Yank.
"Come in," replied the Canuck.

Q. What does the average Canadian think of LSD?
A. That he was an OK President.

Q. How do French Canadians celebrate the 24th of June?
A. They riot in the streets.

Q. How do English Canadians celebrate the 1st of July?
A. They litter the highways.

Q. What do you do if you're living in Ottawa and you want to have a good time?
A. Move.

Q. Is Toronto really "The Philadelphia of Canada"?
A. Absolutely not. Philadelphia is "The Toronto of the U.S."

Q. If they call Russia's border defenses "The Iron Curtain," what do they call Canada's?
A. "The Red Carpet."

Q. Why are Albertans so attached to their oil?
A. They still believe it's the best way to keep hair in place.

Q. What do you do for excitement in Ottawa?
A. Go down to the Dominion and watch the trucks unload...

Q. What is "direct action" in Ottawa?
A. Setting up a committee to investigate the possibility of a Royal Commission.

Q. What rhymes with Canada?
A. Nothing.

> "...The Maple Leaf Newsreel marches into Canada, and marches back out — with nothing to declare."
> — Bruce McCall, "The National Lampoon Radio Hour"

Q. What is the Canadian substitute for adrenaline?
A. Alcohol.

2. How to Tell You're a Canadian at Heart - 100 Test Questions

1. Do you still think that sports cars are ostentatious? *y*

2. Are you overly fond of wearing blue blazers with crests *yes* on the pocket?

3. Do you dream of winning the Loto and buying your own railroad car? *yes*

4. Do you still feel that all braless women are promiscuous? *no*

5. Are you troubled when you hear a man use a four-letter word? *yes*

6. Are you shocked when you hear a WOMAN use a four-letter word? *yes*

7. Have you entered 10 or more sweepstakes in the last year? *no*

8. Do you believe that McDonald's restaurants are just a passing fad?

9. Is it important to you that your car has whitewalls?

10. Can you name every Jewish family living within a 10-block radius of your house?

11. Have you ever lost sleep after running a stop sign?

12. Do you think naughty thoughts every time you hear the word "organ"?

13. Are you ashamed of the fact that you own, or would like to own, property in Florida?

14. Have you ever signed the same chain letter twice?

15. Do you believe Nixon was "railroaded"?

16 Would you ask Joey Smallwood for an autograph?

17. Are you still hoping that George Knudson will finally win a PGA tournament?

18. Do you wear a miniature maple leaf in your buttonhole when you travel abroad?

19. Do you still cringe when you hear someone split an infinitive?

20. Have you ever had the urge to report a jaywalker?

21. Do you still iron Perma-Prest clothes?

22. Is your favorite type of pizza "plain"?

23. Do you still get choked up when you hear Guy Lombardo play "Auld Lang Syne"?

24. Do you feel your wallet whenever a black man walks past you?

25. Do you think it was David Brinkley who impersonated Harvey Kirck, instead of vice versa?

26. Can you get interested in a hockey game between Minnesota and St. Louis?

27. Do you still catch **Front Page Challenge** when the kids are out of the house?

28. Do you still think that George "The Human Punching Bag" Chuvalo was a "helluva fighter" after a few drinks?

29. Do you still refer to drunks as "stoned"?

30. Do you still consider taking the wrong highway exit as an "adventure"?

31. Do you need a new set of brakes twice a year?

32. When you go into a darkened elevator, do you still hesitate to hit the "light on" switch without permission?

33. Do you receive *Plain Truth* in the mail each month?

34. Do you still refuse, as a matter of conscience, to buy a German or Japanese car?

35. Do you sit in the middle of a bench intended for two or three people?

36. Are you still hesitant to buy a can of tuna fish, lest it be tainted?

37. (Male OR female) Do you still get embarrassed at the check-out counter with a box of Tampax?

38. Do you own a hand buzzer?

39. Have you ever gone to the airport just to watch the planes land?

40. Do you still see the train as a technological marvel?

41. Do you think Russians are snappy dressers?

42. Do you spend a lot of time talking about your TV antenna?

43. After a few drinks, do you touch people a lot while talking to them?

44. Do you own any lawn ornaments?

45. Have you ever started a conversation with a wrong number?

46. Can you quickly recite a litany of 100 reasons why Canadian winters aren't so bad?

47. Do your plants die after you talk to them?

48. Do you find people in your office more intrigued by the Muzak than by your conversation?

49. Are you ashamed to go near a mirror when you're nude?

50. Have you ever attended an open house just to kill time?

51. Do you know all the words to the second verse of "The Star-Spangled Banner"?

52. Do you have buried somewhere at least 100 back issues of *Popular Mechanics*?

53. Can you tell at least three anecdotes about bursting water pipes?

54. Do you distrust left-handers?

55. Have you ever planned a vacation around a newspaper ad?

56. While watching TV, do you regularly employ the phrase, "He's a Canadian, eh? "?

57. Do you always stop to read newspaper stories about The Royal Family?

58. Do you average two funerals a week?

59. Do you feel that London is the most exciting city in the world?

60. Are you easily embarrassed by mattress commercials?

61. Do you feel like you're a better person after reading *Reader's Digest*?

62. Do you still feel a little sad that the Union Jack was left off the Canadian flag?

63. Do you still get a tingle up your spine whenever you get a letter addressed to "Occupant"?

64. Do you think that athletes play poorly when they have sex before a game?

65. Do you leave your TV on the same channel all evening?

66. Do you carry two sets of jumper cables in your car?

67. Do you wash your hands BEFORE using the toilet?

68. Do you own a lot of James Last LP's?

69. Do you find yourself crossing the border a lot?

70. Do you still subscribe to *Esquire*?

71. Have you used the word "Negro" in the last 12 months?

72. Do you spend a lot of time worrying about your oil filter?

73. Has anyone ever called you an "old fart"?

74. Are you easily offended by unshined shoes?

75. Do you consider people over 40 as "over the hill"?

76. Have a lot of your co-workers been laid off lately?

77. Have you completely forgotten your childhood?

78. Have you ever had dinner guests fall asleep?

79. Have you ever ordered anything by mail from New Jersey?

80. Is your favorite actress June Allyson?

81. Have you lately used the phrase, "Cold enough for you?"?

82. Do you slow down your car at an accident?

83. Do you still get AM and FM confused?

84. Do you wonder if Gitanes are legal?

85. Do you ask for receipts for 25-cent tolls?

86. (Male) Do you secretly have the "hots" for Helen Hutchinson?

87. (Female) Is your idea of a "Dream Date" a night on the town with George Finstad?

88. Do you think Mary Tyler Moore is a militant feminist?

89. Do you think Quebecois eat their young alive?

90. Do you still glance through the minor-hockey standings and results?

91. Have you ever wanted to write something on a washroom wall, but couldn't think of anything to say?

92. Do you still feel the urge to beat other cars away from a traffic light?

93. Do you still cheer when someone on radio or television mentions your home town?

94. Do you distrust anyone whose last name ends with a vowel?

95. Would you rather buy three cans of peas priced 3/85 than a pair priced 2/50?

96. Do you think you're "living dangerously" every time you turn a burner to High?

97. Have you ever ordered an Export Ale in Germany or Milwaukee?

98. When you're sitting in a movie theater and someone new enters, do you find yourself unable to resist the temptation to look at him?

99. Have you ever thrown a rubber at a hockey game?

100. Do you still get a lump in your throat when they play "O Canada" at a hockey game in the U.S.?

> *Each day, in every way, I am getting more and more indistinguishable.*

Scoring: Count each "yes."

90 - 100 — Next to you, Pierre Berton is a wetback.

80 - 90 — You were still shocked when your fourth consecutive Ford rusted out.

70 - 80 — You spend a lot of time in buildings which prominently display pictures of the Queen.

60 - 70 — You didn't feel too guilty about your Florida vacation last year.

50 - 60 — You're trying to get the Winnipeg concession for Burger King.

40 - 50 — You like pro basketball.

30 - 40 — You have relatives in Oklahoma.

20 - 30 — You've been trying for five years to move to L.A.

10 - 20 — You feel like a stranger in his native land.

0 - 10 — You fought in Vietnam, despite your citizenship.

None right — You have sun-bleached blond hair, you surf and chase women all day while collecting welfare, you love tacos and rhythm and blues.

The only thing we have to fear is getting scared.

3. Good Sports

Q. What's the motto of the Canadian Olympic team?
A. "Winning isn't everything."

Q. What's their battle cry?
A. "We're number 16! "

> *Millions for defense but not one cent for a back-up goaler!*

Q. Where will the Expos finish this year?
A. At the top of the American League West.

Q. Cite an example of Canada's flair for promotion.
A. Their equivalent to the Super Bowl is the Grey Cup.

Q. In which Olympics did Canuck athletes fare the best?

A. The Special Olympics.

Q. What is a Canadian "Olympic hero"?
A. A guy who finished 18th in the pentathlon.

Q. How much money did Bobby Orr make in Boston?
A. Well, he had an unlisted Zip Code number.....

Q. Why do goalies have such big pads?
A. They make such good bread.

Q. What's another name besides "imports" for American players on a CFL team?
A. The "nucleus."

Blessed are the meek, for they shall inherit my season tickets.

Q. What will the Expos' "magic number" be on Sept. 1 of this season?
A. "1988."

Q. Why did they hold the Grey Cup game in Calgary a few years back?
A. The top of Mount Everest was already booked.

The young defenseman and team bully-"policeman" showed up 15 minutes late for hockey practice.
"Just for being late," the coach reprimanded the rookie from Flin Flon, "skate an extra lap around the ice."
A half-hour later, the hulking youngster was still panting around the rink. "What happened? " the coach asked.
"I lost count," he replied.

30

Q. How does a Canadian father know his son might be an NHL prospect?
A. He comes home with his face stitched together.

Q. What do you call an NHL'er with a grade-school education?
A. An "egghead."

Q. Is hockey a violent game?
A. Ask any one-eyed former player.

Q. How do you know the crowds are surly in Maple Leaf Gardens?
A. Where else do they boo the invocation?

Q. If hockey were outlawed, what would be Canada's national sport?
A. Roller derby.

Q. What's another name for a hockey "policeman"?
A. A "felon."

Q. What's the referee signal for a kick in the groin?
A. A shrug of the shoulders.

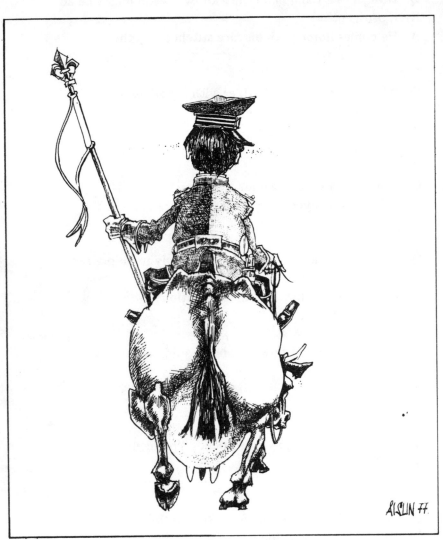

THE NATIONAL QUEBEC MOUNTED POLICE?

Q. What's more ridiculous than the Canadian Army?
A. A Quebec Army.

4. Canadian Headlines

Quebec Volunteer Workers' Strike in 80th Day

Canadian Desk in U.S. State Department Vacated, To Be Used in Amy Carter's School

Radio Programmers Term CRTC's 90-Percent CanCon Rule 'Excessive'

Quebec Birth Rate Down, Levesque Government Cites Technique

Saskatchewan Missing for Third Straight Day; Officials Baffled

Sinclair Heart Attack on 'Front Page Challenge' Attacked as Ratings Ploy

Canadian Decision to Recognize Belgium Termed 'Provocative'

Canada Decision to Sell Idi Amin Plutonium Questioned

Levesque's Appointment of Chiropractor as Ambassador to Russia Questioned

St. John's Premiere of 'Gone With the Wind' Termed Success

Expos Ground Crew Quits, Cites Increasing Use of Nuclear Explosives to Prepare Infield as 'Hazard'

Bethlehem Natives Prepare Holiday Pilgrimage to Trudeau Birthplace

Trudeau Says of Latest Polls: 'What Fools These Mortals Be'

Christmas Slaying Brings Year's Total in P.E.I. to Two

C.I.A. Detachment in Canada Discusses His Role

Supporting Structure Around CN Tower Nears Completion

Air Canada Windsor-Detroit Route Questioned

Cultural Minister Claims, 'Arts in Canada Aren't Dead; They Just Smell Funny'

Trudeau Report to Liberal National Convention: 'I Did It My Way'

Carter Pardons Canadians for Expansion Hockey

Expos Take Over Last Place After Win

Joe Clark Joins Harron as 'Hee Haw' Regular

P.E.I. Gets Liberian Registry

Ron Basford Declines TV Cop Role

Calgary Stampede Injures Bystanders at Bay Day

CBC Cancels 'The National': Cites 'Lack of Interest'

Players Nix CFL Plan to Play Doubleheaders

Levesque Declines Ringling Bros. Offer

Knievel Rejects Offer to Traverse Decarie Blvd. as 'Too Risky'

Diefenbaker Termed 'Forgotten, But Not Gone'

Premier Davis Discusses His 'Roots'

Canadians Sweep Honors at Pillsbury Bake-Offs

Canadian Team Finishes

Drapeau on Deficit: 'I'm Off to See the Wizard'

Enoch Powell Appointment as Governor-General Hailed in Toronto

B.C. Orders Return of All Properties Confiscated from Japanese Canadians in WWII; Half of Vancouver to Change Hands

Peace Tower Clock Strikes Three; Two Escape With Minor Injuries

Harvard Initiates Canadian Studies Course; Students Come Disguised as Empty Seats

Q. What two things do you have to do to make a phone call in St. John's?
A. First, crank; second, talk to Sarah.

5. The National Time Warp

Q. Why is there no 50's nostalgia in Canada?
A. You can't be nostalgic about the present.

Q. Name some trends that are likely to catch on in Canada in the 1980's.
A. CB radio, soul music, push-button telephones, Dr. Pepper.

Q. What is "women's lib" in Canada?
A. Not having to wash the dishes until after **Ozzie and Harriet.**

Q. What is the Canadian equivalent to The National Geographic Society?
A. The Flat Earth Society.

Q. What was the best-selling car in Canada's history?
A. The DeSoto.

Q. What's a "political radical" in Canada?
A. A guy who endorses the Industrial Revolution.

Q. Why hasn't Canada launched its own ICBM yet?
A. They haven't been able to scrape up enough firewood.

Q. How is the show **Happy Days** characterized in most Canadian TV schedules?
A. As "science fiction."

Q. How does Canada's *TV Guide* describe **The Flintstones**?
A. As "contemporary comedy."

Q. What is Calgary's civil defense plan in case of nuclear attack?
A. "First, get the wagons in a circle..."

Q. What's a "hippie" called in Canada?
A. A "beatnik."

Q. Canada is best represented by which cartoon character?
A. Clark Kent.

Q. What time is it in Regina when it's 12 noon in New York?
A. 1951.

Q. Where did they get the inspiration for the new CBC logo?
A. From a dashboard ornament on a Chrysler Airflow.

THE ROYAL CANADIAN MOUNTED
POLICE ALWAYS GET:
☐ their man?
☐ their horse?
☐ the trots?

AISLIN

Q. What's the origin of the Mounties' saying, "We always get our man"?

A. In frontier days, there weren't many women...

Q. What do you call a black person in Regina?
A. A "tourist."

6. People of the Negro and Asian Persuasion

Q. What do most Canadians think of when you mention the expression, "The Great White Hope"?
A. Sickle cell anemia.

Q. How do Canadian students refer to Mahatma Gandhi?
A. As a "towel-head."

Q. How do Torontonians greet a Pakistani?
A. "Vishnu with you? "

Little boy to father in Toronto: "Daddy, are French Canadians and Jews white people? "
Father: "Well, kind of..."

Q. What do they call a Puerto Rican in Canada?
A. Persona non grata.

Q. How can you spot a Canadian at a cocktail party?
A. He's the one who tells a black man, "Some of my best Negroes are friends."

Q. What's Canada's latest joke craze?
A. Sikh "humour."

A Pakistani comes up to a stranger on the street in Toronto and asks him, "Do you have the time, please — or would you like me to fuck off?"

Q. What's the first thing a Canadian does to show his good intentions to an East Indian?
A. He offers to buy him a steak dinner.

Q. Are the Indians in Western Canada really that poor?
A. In most of their homes, if you don't wake up with an erection on Christmas morning, you have nothing to play with all day.

> *"It occurs to me that Canada's national life has been insufficiently troubled."*
> — U.S. Sen. Daniel Patrick Moynihan, addressing Canadians' fears of separatism

CANADIAN CUISINE

"A country often has a distinctive ingredient which distinguishes its cuisine from others. For example, France has cheese. Italy has tomato sauce. In Canada the thing that distinguishes its cooking is ... starch. Every properly equipped Canadian kitchen also has an appliance called a Blander."
— Courtesy, "National Lampoon"

Q. What has replaced "Hogtown" as Toronto's nickname?
A. Toronto the Adequate.

7. The State of the Provinces

Q. What's the most popular deodorant in the Yukon?
A. They scotch-tape pine cones to their armpits.

Q. What was the most-asked question on Toronto talk shows during the FLQ crisis?
A. "Is James cross? "

Q. What's the leading youth organization in North Bay?
A. "A.A."

Q. Why do they call Ottawa a small town?
A. Both city-limits signs are on the same pole.

Q. Why do men in the Northwest Territories drink so much?
A. So they'll be in fighting trim for the evening's chain-saw fights.

Q. What do Quebec mothers tell their children before letting them go outside and play?
A. "Be careful. Premier Levesque may be driving."

Q. What's the FLQ's latest terrorist weapon?
A. The postcard bomb.

Q. What do the dates 1776, 1867 and 1967 have in common?
A. They're adjacent rooms in the Chateau Frontenac in Quebec City.

Q. Why did so many Nova Scotians move from North Sydney to Wolfville in 1940?
A. They wanted to get farther away from the war.

Q. What's the bilingual word for Vancouver?
A. "Terminus."

Q. Why wouldn't Prairie farmers use wheat as a weapon?
A. They tried it, and it makes lousy bullets.

Q. Did you realize that Passover is a Quebecois holiday?
A. Sure — didn't you ever hear one say, "De las' time I pass over dere..."?

Q. What's the name of the movie they're making about Quebec after separation?
A. "Mon Oncle Sam."

Q. What do you call an organization that opens a new office in Montreal?

A. The Quebec Government.

Q. What happened after the Parti Quebecois announced it was getting rid of all English civil servants?

A. There was a net loss of three jobs.

Q. Is it true that Westerners don't like eastern Canadians?

A. Ever heard of the proposed state of North Montana?

Q. What's the big sport in small Alberta towns?

A. Watching the local wino having delirium tremens.

Q. What do you have to do to get a Quebec driver's license?

A. Eat all the caramel popcorn first.

Q. How does one qualify to become a member of Canada's Supreme Court?

A. Be a corporation lawyer specializing in drainage and seepage law.

Q. What's the quickest way to spot a Quebec driver?

A. He tries to start the car by putting the key in the glove compartment.

Q. How can you tell when there's been a major power failure in Montreal?

A. Hydro-Quebec crewmen are out going door-to-door, distributing pennies.

Q. What will be the colors of Quebec's independence flag?
A. 'Le Gang' green and unforeseeable fuchsia.

Q. What makes Hamilton so unique?
A. It's the only city where the birds cough.

Q. Why does Canada have an army?
A. Because it's fashionable.

Q. What are the three gradings of Quebec meat?
A. Win, place, show.

Q. How does the average Calgarian see Archie Bunker?.
A. As a Renaissance Man.

OTTAWA "HUMOUR"

Q. How does a civil servant wink?
A. He opens one eye.

Q. Why don't civil servants look out their windows in the morning?
A. They need something to do in the afternoon.

CANADIAN OBSERVATIONS

Frailty, thy name is Confederation.

* * *

There are no answers, only question periods.

* * *

United we stand, divided we'll manage.

* * *

Physician, bill thyself! — Medicare

* * *

Possession is against the law.

* * *

Ask not what your country can do for you, but ask what you can do to get out of it.

* * *

Canadian genius is 10 percent imitation and 90 percent importation.

Q. What's Drapeau's next planned extravaganza?
A. Prince Charles' coronation.

Q. ...and if that doesn't work out?
A. The St. Lawrence River will put on a colorful display as it bursts into flames.

8. Rated "X"

Q. What two things do most Canadian girls aspire to?
A. 1) Swimming Lake Ontario; 2) after they've developed the necessary muscular physique, becoming Air Canada stewardesses.

Q. Why does the Canadian government pay its people to have babies?
A. They wouldn't think of it otherwise.

Q. How do most Canadian males regard sex?
A. As a blank on an application form.

Q. What do they do with prostitutes arrested in Canada?
A. Sew an "A" on their dresses.

Q. What do men and women do in bed in Canada?
A. Sleep.

Canadian to his wife during their monthly lovemaking session: "What's the matter, dear? Did I hurt you?"
Wife: "No, why?"
Canadian: "You moved."

WARNING

You cannot play LP's on a Francophone. Or pornography, either. For that, you need a pornograph.

Q. Is it true that there was a TV series about Canadian honeymoons?
A. Yes, it was called, "Emission: Impossible."

Q. What's the Canadian definition of "oral sex"?
A. Telling dirty jokes.

Q. What do they call an unwed mother in New Brunswick?
A. Names.

Q. What does a lumberjack use for an opening line in a Vancouver singles bar?
A. "I'm so horny the crack of dawn isn't safe around me."

Q. What's the Quebec way of getting a "quickie" divorce?
A. Arson.

Q. How can you tell if a guy's from the Yukon?
A. He looks like a husky fucker.

> *"The future growth of English in Quebec is up to the power of your loins."*
> Rene Levesque (*The Gazette*, Montreal, March 21, 1977)

Canada's weather is so bad, people jump INTO burning buildings.

9. Iso Bars

It was so cold today in Toronto, I saw people standing next to Betty Kennedy for warmth.

Q. How do you take your clothes off in Canada?
A. With an ice pick.

> *If you can't stand the heat, turn the thermostat down.*

Q. How do gangsters in the Northwest Territories "rub out" someone?
A. They take him "for a walk" in January.

Q. What precaution do you have to take on Canadian nights?
A. You have to bring all your brass monkeys indoors.

Q. Why are Canada's streets so safe at night?
A. Because no one else is stupid enough to be out.

Q. Why was the Metric System such a "great idea"?
A. Now, instead of being 10 degrees, it's -11.

"The weather will keep Canada out of The Big Time."
— Les Sole, Canadian broadcaster

"*Culture in Canada exists in a strictly anthropological sense.*"
— Author unknown

57

CANADA IS:
☐ true?
☐ false?

10. A Canadian View of History

1456 Gutenberg's first Bible published: "Isn't that a division of Southam's? "

1536 Anne Boleyn executed: "Wasn't Genevieve Bujold great in that part? "

1814 British troops burn White House: "They had it coming to them for their disgraceful conduct toward George III."

1815 Napoleon defeated by Wellington at Waterloo: "Christopher Plummer was great in that part. He's a Canadian, you know..."

1836 All defenders die at The Alamo: "Couldn't ANY of them speak Spanish, for goodness sake? "

1848 Gold discovered in California: "...and you see what's happened to the place..."

1860 Abraham Lincoln elected: "No wonder; he looked even more Lincolnesque than Raymond Massey."

1861 U.S. Civil War begins: "If that didn't prove how violent America is, then I don't know what does..."

1868 D'Arcy McGee shot in first Canadian political assassination: "Actually, he died of lead poisoning."

1876 Custer's "Last Stand": "What was he doing out there in the first place? "

1879 Edison invents electric light: "Wasn't his laboratory in Guelph? "

1885 Louis Riel hanged: "I once heard on TV that he was given a suspended sentence, but that didn't make any sense..."

1903 Wright Brothers' first flight: "Weren't they the two boys from Kingston? "

1914 World War I begins: "And I still get a tingle every time I hear that poem..."

1927 Lindbergh's famous flight: "I heard that he overshot Gander."

1929 The Wall Street "Crash": "My uncle moved to St. John's ... he said they never noticed."

1934 Dionne quints born in Ontario: "We were so proud of them..."

1936 King Edward VIII abdicates: "That's what happens when you run around with those American divorcees..."

1938 Hitler invades Austria: "I never did trust a man with a mustache..."

1952 Queen Elizabeth, first monarch enthroned in name of Canada: "We finally had our very own Queen..."

1959 St. Lawrence Seaway opens: "If you ask me, this was more of a step forward than all the satellites in the world."

1961 Abortive Bay of Pigs invasion: "If they had wanted Cuban cigars, they could have come to Toronto."

1963 Kennedy murdered: "That's what happens when you venture into the Deep South..."

1965 Watts race riots: "You didn't see that sort of thing going on up HERE! "

1969 Jets upset Colts in thrilling Super Bowl: "We still have the best rules and game..."

1974 Nixon resigns: "The Jews and Negroes finally got to him."

1975 U.S. final withdrawal from Vietnam: "My gosh, I hope their returning soldiers don't bring any strange tropical diseases across the border with them."

1976 Jimmy Carter elected U.S. President: "That man is always smiling; I don't like that."

I regret that I have only this country to give for my life. —*L. Riel*

Q. Why are the Canadians such a large lobby in Florida?
A. They control most of the state's swampland.

11. Sleeping with King Kong

Q. Why will Canadians like this book?
A. Because Someone Down There noticed.

Q. What, in general, are the most popular Canadian beliefs about Americans?
A. 1) The police all look like Archie Bunker.

2) Most of the people are New York Jews, Boston Irish, Chicago Mafiosi or Mexican cutthroats.

3) Americans are all pushy and carry guns to back it up.

4) All U.S. presidents are assassinated.

5) All of the police-station doors have peepholes.

Q. How can you spot an American driving up to Canada?
A. He has a canoe lashed to his car.

Q. How much significance is there to the raising of the Quebec flag in Florida?
A. About as much as raising the Disneyland banner in New Guinea.

Q. Where can a Canadian find a sympathetic ear after he's been conned out of his money in New York?
A. He should take such complaints to the Minister of Fisheries.

Q. What do most Americans think of Saskatoon?
A. "Do they still use those? "

Q. What is the ŏne natural resource that Canada sadly lacks?
A. Florida or California.

Q. Why do Americans view Canada as a Land of Hope?
A. They hope that the Russians' missiles will run out of fuel over Canadian territory.

Q. What phrase is often used to describe the growing Canadian colony in Los Angeles?
A. "Hollywood Squares."

Q. Why is it a bad idea asking Americans what they think of Canada?
A. Because they're afraid they'll be pestered next by some clown from Ecuador.

My country right or wrong, unless it devalues my house.

Q. What's Canada's leading export to the U.S.?
A. Canadians.

Q. What is the most common Canadian belief about travelling in the U.S.?
A. That you'll either get mugged, raped, robbed, or lynched.

Q. ...and the advice most often given to Yanks travelling to Canada?
A. Better bring along a camera so you have proof for your Congressman that you saw baby seals being slaughtered.

Q. Why can't Yanks sell Canada short?
A. First, you need a buyer...

Q. Give an example of Canadian money being accepted at par value in the U.S.
A. To buy hotels on Boardwalk and Park Place.

Q. Why shouldn't your daughter marry a Canadian?
A. She might have to live there...

Imitation is the sincerest form of Canadianism.

Q. What concerns American tourists in Canada the most?
A. Having their car sideswiped by a covered wagon.

Q. Name a few things Americans think about more often than Canada.

A. Bessemer converters; iguanas; the Periodic Table of Elements; curbstones; cookie cutters; nose hairs.

Q. Why must Canadians pay $500 more on the average for a new car?

A. Because they're built in Canada.

12. Oy Canada

Q. What's the Canadian equivalent of Harvard?
A. There isn't one.

Q. Name a popular, Canadian-produced TV show.
A. The Irish Rovers.

Q. Name some countries that are WORSE business investments than Canada.
A. Tanzania, Uruguay, Zambia, Greenland, Albania, North Korea, Estonia, Latvia, Krakatoa, Bangladesh, Croatia, Cuba, Spanish Sahara, Biafra.

Q. Name some things harder to get than a Canadian passport.
A. A common cold, a bottle of Coke, unsolicited mail.

Q. Name the most popular Canadian-made cars.
A. Ford, Chevrolet, Dodge, Camaro.

Q. Do Canadians closely associate immigrants with cheap labor?
A. Why do you think they call it the Department of Manpower and Immigration?

Q. Why did Lester Pearson win the Nobel Peace Prize in 1957?
A. The Scandinavians got him confused with Ike.

Q. How do Canadian nationalists pay for their lunches?
A. American Express.

Q. Name some Canadian record companies.
A. RCA Records of Canada; Capitol Records of Canada; Motown Records of Canada...

Show me a Canadian with his head held high and I'll show you a man with a very stiff neck.

Q. What's an example of "Canadian nationalism"?
A. Lorne Greene reading "In Flanders Fields" on Remembrance Day — via telephone from Los Angeles. (November 11, 1976)

Q. Why doesn't Air Canada fly at night?
A. You can't see the water towers.

CANADIAN FIRSTS

Don't ever let anyone tell you that Canadians aren't there when history is being made! Some examples:

1870 Thomas A. Edison invents the stock ticker; on Dec. 11 of the same year, John Alcan of Toronto, Ont., becomes the first stockbroker to declare bankruptcy.

1892 Robert Duncan, an American, invents the addressograph. His next-door neighbor was a Canadian.

August 15, 1921 John Dough of Peace River, Alta., becomes the first man to be overcharged on an electric cash register.

1927 Babe Ruth hits his historic 60th home run in Yankee Stadium. The ball strikes John Broadfeet of Sudbury, Ont., in the head.

1933 John Hookline Andsinker of Kenora, Ont., becomes the first person to be struck by lightning twice in the same week.

1951 Jean-Guy Lessard the Fifth of St. Agapit, P.Q., becomes the first person to take his own life with an electric razor.

1954 Dr. Peter Lupus-Lupus of York University writes his precedent-setting paper for *Natural Phenomena* entitled "Did You Ever Wonder What Those Funny-Looking Lights Up North You See in the Summer Were? "

1969 New York Jets upset Baltimore in greatest-ever Super Bowl — without one Canadian on roster!

WHAT COMES TO MIND AT THE MENTION OF CANADIAN FOLKLORE?

☐ Indian totem poles?
☐ eskimo sculpture?
☐ welfare cheques?

* FROG, BEAR, RAVEN, AND CIVIL SERVANT DEVOURING ESKIMO.

AISLIN

Q. Why is Eskimo art so popular in Canada?
A. Because it's the most avant-garde stuff in the country.

13. Culture?

Q. Who is the Canadian equivalent of Burt Reynolds?
A. Fred Davis.

Q. Name one of Canada's current best sellers.
A. "Your Friend, the Entrenching Tool."

Q. Name one good thing about **The Tommy Hunter Show.**
A. It's a great emetic...

Q. What's the CBC-CTV equivalent of the grand prize on
The $20,000 Pyramid?
A. $14.40 cash and a Toast 'R' Oven.

Q. What is worse than death?
A. Only two things: spending an entire evening with an
insurance salesman, and sitting through all 14 parts of the
John Diefenbaker Story on CBC.

THE CANADIANIZING OF POPULAR CULTURE

One can only wonder what would have happened if some of the functionaries at the CBC had been responsible for giving names to some of the popular American shows.

Starsky and Hutch would have become **Mackenzie and Mowat.**

Fish would have become **Ichthyolite.**

Best Sellers might today be **Trade Demographic Trend-Setters.**

Charlie's Angels would have become **Stanfield's Sylphs.**

Soul Train would have become **Afro-Canadian Dance Party.**

Most Wanted would be **The Queen Versus...**

The Gong Show might have been labeled **Assent or Disapprove?**

Kojak would have become **Ballard.**

Hogan's Heroes would be transformed into **Stalag-13: A Diary.**

Good Times might become **Days of Amicability.**

Hitch your wagon to a car.

The Six Million Dollar Man would become **Bionic Humanoid of No Mean Worth.**

Chico and the Man would be called **Jean-Pierre and the Foreman.**

Police Woman would become **Fully Deputized Female Law Enforcement Officer.**

Roots would be metamorphosed into **Rhizomes.**

What's Happening! ! would become **Eh?**

Some shows would need little explanation after their CBC name change:

You'd see such programs as **The Lance Corporal and Tennille;** or popular soaps like **All My Offspring;** quiz shows like **The Valuation is Correct;** and the ABC sports show on weekends called **The Standouts.**

Then there would be **The Unexplained Extraphysical Phenomenon and Mrs. Muir; Non-Domestic Kingdom; The $91.08 Trihedron; Space:1963;** and **Moderately Pleasant Days.**

CBC would also have sure winners like **Hollywood Trapezoids; Satisfactory Performances; The Novice Patrolmen; Saturday Evening Only Partly on Film;** and, of course, the ever-popular **All in the Nuclear Domestic Grouping.**

All the world's a stage; and all the men and women are union.

CANADIAN INVENTIONS AND DISCOVERIES

Canadians are responsible for inventing and/or discovering the following:

enriched bread
Pringle's Potato "Chips"
the Whoopee cushion
the asterisk
the paper clip
the electric can opener
flamingo lawn ornaments
cross-checking
the ampersand
the crescent wrench
Kellogg's Pop Tarts
the Packard Clipper
the toilet float
the word "mundane"
parcheesi
the flesh-colored crayon
the Veg-o-matic
the 48-rpm record
pistachio ice cream
clip-on bow ties
gravel
Carter's Little Liver Pills
Feen-a-Mint
the 222
rubber stamps
power windows
the motorized wheelchair
button-down collars
the marimba
the heartbreak of psoriasis
white slavery

→ DRESS LIKE A NEW YORKER.
→ TALK LIKE A NEW YORKER.
→ DRINK LIKE A NEW YORKER.
→ READ THE NEW YORKER.
→ HATE NEW YORK.
→ HATE THE C.B.C.
→ WORK FOR THE C.B.C.

Q. What's the most often seen show on the CBC?

A. "Technical difficulties."

IF-CANADIANS-HAD-NAMED-THE-MOVIES DEPARTMENT

You'd see films with names like —

Strong Disagreement on the Bounty

The Noteworthy Ziegfeld

The Satisfactory Earth

Gone With the 30-km. Westerlies

Going My Direction

Around the World in 80 Days — on AC Flight 500

To Incapacitate a Mockingbird

Which Minority-Group Member is Joining Us for Dinner?

A Man for Both Seasons

Murder on the Rapido

Air Terminal 1975

Earthtremor

Once is Too Much

(Kitchener)-Waterloo

Moose Jaws

North by North Bay

Q. Is **The National** really completely worthless?
A. No. It makes a great night light.

Q. In which category do Canadians win the most Oscars?
A. Short subjects.

Q. What's the Canadian equivalent of the pop group Chicago?
A. The Carleton Showband.

Q. What's a good description of the CBC?
A. "The heartbeat of mediocrity."

Q. Why can't the CBC drop **Front Page Challenge**?
A. They're still negotiating for the rights to **Industry on Parade** and **Make That Spare**.

Q. Name a popular Canadian TV serial.
A. **Coronation Street.**

The moving finger writes/and, having writ,/gets a painful cramp.

Q. What line best describes the Canadian government's heavy subsidization of the arts?

A. "While you're up, get me a grant."

14. Assorted Canada Council Grants, 1977-78

$300,000 — for Toronto Symphony to play a concert of Bach selections in the Royal Gander Airport, July 1 - 3.

$21,000 — to D'Arcy McGee H.S. chorale, Vancouver, for their trip to Bucharest to perform selections from "Frampton Comes Alive."

$15,000 — to Andre LaSchmuck, Trois-Rivieres, P.Q., for a feasibility study on Quebec Council Grants.

$45,000 — to La Ligue des Patriotes de Rosemont, P.Q., for their four-act play, "Mange d'la merde, les maudits anglais d'Ottawa! "

$50,000 — to the Video Cooperative of Cote St. Luc, P.Q., for feasibility studies toward making a one-hour documentary on underbooked Air Canada flights to Acapulco.

$5,675 — to Darnley Chillworth-Kensington III, Calgary, Alta., for his research on the cultural impact of luxury automobiles passing quickly through Cree Indian reservations.

$5,500 — to Penticton, B.C. cellist Isaac Urns, because his name sounded familiar.

$15,600 — to the Joe Louis, P.Q. Public School to create an abstract sculpture out of 13,000 Mae Wests.

$10,500 — to Shawnigan Lake, B.C. Community College, for readings by Xavier Cugat.

$5,000 — to Tech. Sgt. I.B. Damd, of RCAF Base Ground Zero, for his collection of essays on "The Impact of Fresh Produce Dropped on Selected Alberta Venues from a Height not Exceeding 30,000 Feet."

$300 — to "Occupant," General Delivery, N.W.T., for successfully filling out his initial form to the Council.

$4,000 — to Les Editions Diet Rite, Ville Lasalle, P.Q., for the publication of 15 works in the past 12 months dealing with snowmobile safety.

$4,500 — to Goon Lake, B.C. poet Althea Ifitsore, for her volume, "Trilogy — Four Poems."

$3,000 — to Guano Lake, Sask. Community College, for a reading by Martha Raye.

$5.75 — to Ottawa cabbie Max Hulk, for his vocal presentation, "My Meter Is Still Running, Jerk."

$10,000 — to Toronto, Ont. group Discount Bin to help finance their third comeback.

$4,500 — to Les Editions Kik, Montreal, P.Q., for the development of a Braille dictionary in joual.

$100,255 — to the Edmonton Symphony, to fly to England to look for Procol Harum.

$15,500 — to Jean-Guy Gonzales, Verdun, P.Q., for his reading entitled "J'ai lu le *Montreal-Matin* aujourd'hui; demain, je vais lire *Le Journal de Montreal.*"

$10,000 — to John Dunce, Toronto, Ont., for his 16mm film, "Elwood Glover Remembers."

$3,000 — to Tommy Typo, Ottawa, Ont., for his book, "Journalism — Literature in a Hurry."

$50 — to Chuck U. Farley, Hamilton, Ont. Jr. High, so that he may complete his essay entitled, "How I Spent My Summer."

$4,000 — to Floyd English, Cornwall, Ont., for his book entitled, "Separatism: Threat or Menace? "

$450,000 — to the St. Catharines, Ont. Symphony, just for asking for it.

$75,000 — to Montreal, P.Q. author Mortuary Tickler, for the use of his name on Page 3.

$5,000 — to the Kingston, Ont. Penitentiary Writer Co-op for a documentary on the last prison riot.

$30,000 — to Moncton, N.B. poet I.M. Turkey for his work-in-progress, "Golden Reflections on Lithographic Onanism."

$30,560 — to the Rosedale, N.S. Hemiplegic Association, for their performance of "Wheelchairs on Ice."

$50,000 — to "Occupant," General Delivery, N.W.T., for his work, "Successful Obfuscations in Fiduciary Funding Form-Completion."

$4,000 — to The Poets Workshop, Anomie, Nfld., for refilling a prescription of Valium during works-in-progress.

$108,000 — to establish a Community Theater on Floating Island T-34 in Hudson Bay.

$7,500 — to Field Marshal Klaus E. Schickelgruber (Ret.), listed address "Bunker D-78, Alberta," for his book, "The Urgence of Implementing National Socialism in Alberta."

$55,000 — to The Mormon Tabernak Choir, Jonquiere, P.Q., for their cantata, "Les Grands Succès d'Elvis."

$5,500 — to Hamilton, Ont. entertainer Ron E. Whatfor for his recital, "Gimme the fucking money — or you better have your goddam bags packed."

$30,000 — to the Cote St. Luc, P.Q. Video Cooperative for a continuous 18-hour film study of a traffic light at the corner of Crescent and Dorchester Sts., Montreal.

$100,000 — in miscellaneous costs for the Canada Council booklet.

$5,000 — to Peter Out, of Thorndale, Ont., for his collection of essays on avant-garde crop rotation techniques.

$40,000 — for a performance of the Montreal Symphony at the Mackay Center for the Deaf.

$15,500 — to the Film Cooperative of Beanblossom, N.S., to make an 18-minute documentary on the city's comfort stations.

$2,000 — to Lt. R.U. Conscious for his three-act drama, "Stalemate at Dieppe."

$4,000 — to industrialist Cyrus Eaton for his book, "Quick Money-Making Ideas."

$5,100 — to Arnie Gold, Hampstead, P.Q., for his study of memorable Wayne & Shuster "bits."

$300,000 — to the Toronto Symphony for a trip to play "An Evening of Sibelius" for the people of "Trenchtown," Kingston, Jamaica.

$5,000 — to Jake Yarmulke, Toronto, Ont., for his study of the impact of Canadian culture on a typical U.S. community (West Palm Beach, Fla.).

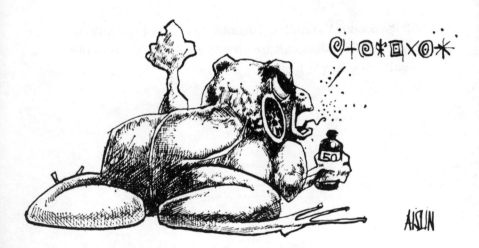

Q. What is a punch line called in French?
A. "Un paragraphe."

15. A Glossary of Canadian Media Usage

"Exciting" can refer to:

The Beachcombers
cloud formations
hockey line changes
newly installed traffic lights
a sudden rise in the barometric pressure
new colors of CIL paints
Davey Keon
opera-window options on a Buick
Diane Stapley
The Stampeders
the "new" Calgary
The Royal Highlanders Tattoo
new options on the Registered Retirement Savings Plan
the new Toronto air terminal
the St. Lawrence Seaway
a new postal issue
GE Soft-Lite bulbs
Squeeze Parkay
vinyl tops

"Awesome" is used in regard to:

the CN Tower
a shorthanded goal
3-D movies
"Earthquake"
high-speed elevators
Wilt Chamberlain
a Pepsi bottling plant
microwave ovens
"Roots"
the new line of Ford LTD's
the Olympic Stadium
the Olympic deficit
Kathy Kreiner's Olympic performance
the Seattle Space Needle

"Magnificent" refers to:

Disneyland
Lester Pearson
Rocket Richard's 500th goal
the Toronto subway system
the Vancouver skyline
Upstairs, Downstairs
a hard-hitting Charles Lynch column
any come-from-behind hockey win
Ferguson Jenkins
"Cabaret"
Banff
the Rapido
"The National Dream"
Farley Mowat's ego
Alistair Cooke's **America**
the Queen's Christmas Message

"Provocative" is used preceding:

panty hose
face-lifts
above-the-knee hemlines
the word "damned"
long hair
Farrah Fawcett-Majors
the Mercury Montego
the Philadelphia-Camden metropolitan area
"Alice Doesn't Live Here Anymore"
oral contraceptives
frozen waffles
TV douche ads
Barbara Walters
George Sand
Maude
Princess Margaret
Pierre Trudeau
singles bars
Catherine Deneuve
Doris Day
Joe Namath
Jade East
racing stripes
jockey-type underwear
any braless woman
Esquire
CP Air stewardesses' uniforms
the color pink
cucumbers
psychedelically-lit bars
Mary Hartman
the words:
        "eunuch"
        "penetrate"
        "excrete"

"washroom"
"throbbing"
"female"
"ripe"
"colostomy"
"sheep"

"Controversial" refers in Canada to:

Yoga
transcendental meditation
dental medication
jazz
beatniks
work slowdowns
daylight saving time
coed dormitories
Johnny Carson
convertibles
X-rays
fluoridation
natural childbirth
yogurt
"M*A*S*H"
feminism
sex-education courses
Darwin's Theory of Evolution
Sesame Street
computers
pre-marital sex
beards
no-fault insurance
CB radio
hydroponic gardening
mouth-to-mouth resuscitation

the Beatles
John Diefenbaker
lower-case headlines
"Peanuts"
Water Piks
"glitter-rock"
Margaret Thatcher
crunchy peanut butter
Christine Keeler
filter-tip cigarettes
Prince Charles
bilingualism
bisexuality
anything starting with "bi-", including "bicycling"

"New" in the media often refers to:

color television
capital gains taxes
homicide
colored people
felt-tip pens
major league baseball
freeze-dried coffee
indoor tennis
crooked doctors
female orgasms
inflation
national disunity
sliced bread (Maritimes only)
nervous tension
UHF TV
nuclear power
cynicism
push-button phones
Name That Tune

"Unique" in Canada refers to:

Canadian sports heroes
CBC programs with more than a 10 share of audience
people speaking French in Vancouver
Jewish comics
people who wear string ties
80-degree days in May
MP's who are distinguishable from their rostrums

"Innovative" in Canada refers to:

digital watches
air-conditioned buildings
Gordon Lightfoot songs
any Canadian novel
Anne Murray's vocal style
air-cooled engines
Air Canada reservations computers
concrete dams

"Sexy" in the minds of Canadians best describes:

Betty Kennedy
Ford Thunderbirds
Mary Tyler Moore
Robert Q. Lewis
Peter Gzowski
Jacques Cousteau
Dick Cavett
Morley Safer
Arthur Murray
Charles Aznavour
Laverne & Shirley

Alistair Cooke
Ben Wicks
Julie Andrews
William Shatner
power windows
Neil Diamond LP's
Myron Floren
Quebec Bonds at 9 3/4 percent
Jackie Gleason albums with Bobby Hackett
Russ Jackson
"Scenes from a Marriage"
psychiatrists
Gisele MacKenzie
trains entering tunnels
Tatum O'Neal

"Obscene" is used before mention of:

Penthouse
Jerry Rubin
Linda Lovelace
most blacks
"Fritz the Cat"
The Fonz
all Henry Miller books
see-thru nighties
tight jeans
hula dancers
flagpoles
Elvis
Alice Cooper
rock and roll
California

"Disgusting" refers to:

Hustler
separatists
Xaviera Hollander
Truman Capote
all homosexuals
Communists
oral sex
Pakis
"water sports"
cigars
Jews
the Rolling Stones
all reptiles
Sweathogs
union leaders
Detroit

> *You can fool some of the people all of the time;*
> *all of the people some of the time; but you can't*
> *fool some of the people some of the time.*

CANADA IS:

More powerful than Costa Rica!

More diverse than Wichita, Kansas!

More laughs than a poster child!

Balmier than Greenland!

More spacious than needed!

Q. If Canada were a store, what sign would be hanging in its front window?

A. "Out to Lunch."